LABYRINTH

LABYRINTH

poetry and prose by **Eenam Vang**

atmosphere press

To —,

I cannot remember what the purpose of these words are. Perhaps I do but I'd rather keep these names that have given me a hybrid of heaven and hell on earth unknown. Some have bruised me purposely for the fame of quantity, many left once my existence was better off an absence, and others stripped me to pieces after speaking the truth they claimed false.

Looking back now, I thank them for breaking me and making me realize that in solitude, resides my naiveness in being a late bloomer; a poisoned inked reality that let me dream with eyes wide open, an anthem to stay true to myself.

I've gathered the courage to finally admit my faults in each past mistaken journey in this lifetime. I am the villain in his world, the bad guy in her universe, a-good-for-nothing in their eyes, a robber of hearts in the night, and a temporary living soul. I am a heavy sinner even on my best days.

We are all guilty, charged of a crime, no matter how big or small it is; innocent does not run in our blood. We play life, gambling expectations from movies and false alarmed desires. Perhaps, when I go through these pages again, I'll laugh, even cry, maybe?

In the end, our lives will be cut short, making room for what will soon be ancient. We will be fossils by then, possibly, forgotten?

And for this, you have all of my love. Please, always be human. These words are for you to keep for as long as you breathe.

Yours Truly,
E.

WARNING:
The following contains emotions.
If proceeding,
I dare you to be vulnerable
with me.

For
the late-night musings and longing fancies
that continues to happen in the crook of my hibernating
thoughts.

Contents

Unrequited Chase

I turn you into poetry, making each bruising and metallic stained memory an attempt to picture me in your bloodshed reveries. Only fools unlock kingdoms, dig graves of heads to give two halves of hearts in the sleeves of their teeth to you. Unlike them, I can see the defeat in your aura that resonates so heavenly with mine. We were holding onto strings of temporary promises; our hands in the recovery of time, itself. In finding your treasured chest, comes a woeful past around our lucid dreams. I hate to admit it but I have become selfish, time in my pocket and slowing it down just to be with you awhile more. I have become hopeful that with my presence by your side, it'll be enough to heal your brokenness. Indeed, I have turned you into poetry, my dear but I forgot that the person you were yearning for isn't me.

Flowers in her Hair

Root like red-seedless dandelions
in the halls of summer,
pace and panic;
each blown away wish
upon their parachute ruderals.
Paint and pacify
in acceptance
of the rotting;
a mastery of crack
uncertainty.

Gilded Age

Grasp for air,
                    Once.
Blues in blood and moons of howl,
                        Twice.
Eyes of sun, blinds of white.
                    Careful,
                        my dear.
Tied lips and sealed hands,
                    End this ode,
            this ode of—

One.
Catch.
Your.
Breath.

            *
                        Two.
                Carve your sins in
                tombs and pins.
Sail this tale to the ends of

            Hell.

Dystopia

The city talks too,
says they crave sleep like we do.

Rudimentary Consistency

I begin to wonder why my soul is crept upon wired machines
and coated sugar dreams. Upon the safety of my core distinction,
distant memories remain brutally obstructive to make of anything
I could retrace back to.

Living on my head only gives me remembrance in collected
farewells often said.

My subconsciousness fiend into reality as familiar faces lock me
out of their lives, excusing my existence of a lesson learned or
simply a trial long overdue; better for absence.

I could fathom what I know now and yet, flux still wouldn't be
the answer to the past doings and its incomplete journey.

So, what did you expect when my silence
hurt you more than the weapons on your lips?

Shadowing Limbics

Ashed carcass aligns into the existence
of sheltered stars;
a muse to the start.

Perhaps, it'll meet ends with
its fated coffin someday
and I,
a home
to the living.

Jaded Cruelty

are we ever really saving anyone
when were the ones protecting ourselves
from what we fear to become?

Fatal Carelessness

Create a vision; a limbo in the sun's golden gate.
Such carelessness can burn out the sky
and the underworld, combine.
Seconds turn to minutes,
Rotting to seeds,
Years to moments,
unknown to existence,
and you to me;
here.
Only,
your hands grip onto
the bouquet of carnations.

Befriending Fiends

I cannot afford to let my seldom spoken
demons scare anyone else away.
It should only haunt me.

Sharpen Your Mouth

My bones decode;
they dare point their arsenic
stained fingers at me.
Claim I,
a robber in the rut.

Let me carry the show everywhere I go.
Head held high with gossip upon this
nothing town.

Call for me,
and I will certainly give you the crime
you so gladly
preach about.

When the Night is Over

"Look at us, fancying about each other."
"I know, it's silly."
"We're *both* silly."

Fools and Their Luck

What is fathomed in the circumstances of it all is the distant recalls; a ritual to bidding farewells every time a tell is on sale. I am not enough to make you stay. I know that now. I give more than you need and in exchange, you left every single part of me out of your life, not knowing exactly where to place it.

I can't help but laugh at how foolish I am when it comes to luck and its intricate tricks. It's my fault for thinking that you can handle it. It just never crossed my mind that you could be the wrong person to see the madness of it all.

But now I know.

It terrifies you each time a tell is sold because it is exactly how you bleed.

Demigods

The bass in between our body
drives on bloody roads and blistered
maladies.

Thunder drapes training wheels,
breaking spines in two,
head halves of baby teeth and spoiled
milk.

In demigods,
live we.
Drench in ecstasy,
infinitely, and
eternally.

Hostage

I let her wash my scalp
with lost toys and
bitten-back lies.

I let him nail tool boxes
in my pulse,
energize for false knowledge
when long ago,
they let my imagination run just to
die.

Grab strings
and pull my body
as spies.

My dear,
I'm no damn prize
but all eye see
are I's.

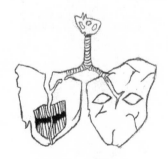

Purgatory Sideline

Frantic are we,
a battle to surviving
the eerie streets.
Often enough,
I forget that each day passing
is another ritual practiced
to Death
in hopes of
an afterlife.

Spoken Tragedy

Words are words.
Sometimes, they cannot fix people.

Wavelength Decisions

In loneliness,
my company is a covet
only past
the a.m. of twelve.
I decipher the air
too thick to clear
despite being
a temporary
wishing well.

Finding a Home Body

I don't think we'll ever get used to the earthly grounds crashing upon hurt and the wolf who cries sunset. Our skins were meant to cease and open wounds of deceiving shelves. The recovery is just a time filter to disguise our ignorance.

Selfish Distractions

I've been catching up with my own headed demons
and walking side by side with their childlike emotions
that I forgot about the dreams that had been embracing me,
oh so tightly.

You are what I live for
            and yet, I wanted more.

                        My dearest apologies.

— x, humans are selfish.

Headspace

"Why do you write?"

"Because you'll get tired of me talking about it."

Molding Skin and Bones

Being built up with caffeine and bags underneath my dark brown light, I didn't know better than the counting of sun kiss poetry dripping down from my chap lips.

There is no such thing as "once upon a time" or "happily ever after"; we both expect too much, maybe?

But here I am; a rabbit hole in the pitfall of reality. It comes with blood of vituperation and aches of justice, unfolding only what seems like colors of pandemonium. You and I seek it as our fairytale deplete.

Perhaps, I am crazy but if it saves you,

I am willing.

A Child's Lullaby

I've done wrong.
Your hands sleep onto mine and
paralyze,
I am.

I *am* the wrong.
Off with my sins and
innocent, not I—
Yes, I
bruise people, skin deep and
root ruins in the grounds of their earth.
Headspace clog my careless teeth to
preach of noxious screams.

Eye awake in the mourn and
condemn a callous
so malevolent.

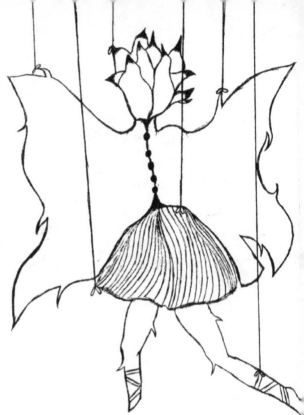

The Masters' Puppet

Blind the fools and
cover me in rose gold lilies.
The light will shine with
glimmers and jewels;
it is them, I pity.

Script me in a play and
depict my glamour
within your rage.

They know better
than to make me a prey,
yet their famish eyes
beg to lock me in
a gilded cage.

Lavished Lifeline

In loving you, my dear sweetheart,
I grasp the errs we build
and in collision,
distance was the cost of
my life.

You keep the receipts
and rip the tags
because I was too cheap
for your damn pride.

Greed of Innocence

What a prisoned gate it is above our hairlines
for the sky to escape acidic streams.
A touch to the skin glides in desperate need of
shelter,
seeping to the burials
of hell.
And yet, here,
comes blooms of
saturated burrow.

Painted Figures

I find myself still grieving over past life nothingness in my mind.

Sky High

The train of raindrops
drown with transparent schemes
and films the earth
with forlorn reveries.

My eyes avert from
the charcoaled black road
and up to the air space control.

Above my existence,
perhaps, a war has been uplifted
in silence.

Lightning roars
and thunder strikes back.
Here, I soak in the taste of salt
and metallic armor liquor
across my busted lips.

A Grand Loss

I lost a friend today, a lover in the moment, and a whole lot of myself. I guess that happens when you commit in the present and don't think of the consequences in their next destination.

Company for Broken Hearts

We see ourselves in others.
The sad. The hurt.
Our past lovers.

We carry all pain to keep us
from going insane.

Our worlds collide and I fall apart,
for I know,
you could never love me
from the start.

So, here's your company
for broken hearts
because to me,
you were my art.

Sadistic Realist

And perhaps this storm will be the only thing that keeps me sane.

The Body's Mistress

She is jet lagged
of mysteries in curiosity,
traveler by feet in her
faraway pipe dream.

Shut eyes stay woke
in night and day, she evokes.

Fingers deep,
flesh bleeding,
her face is finally
peeling.

A Sinner and A Fighter

If angels are pure, I cannot praise them for what they have done for me. They remind me of my naive, undeveloped self—too afraid to live and terrified of death. They lock me out of my own body, silence my heart, and let me cry for help despite knowing that I need a hand to hold.

But up the kill tops of my last breath comes the troops of my demons, a rollercoaster of sinners and duplicates of fiends that have come out to utter a simple greet. They have brought comfort in their rituals and a lullaby to shush my weep in the making. They have given me their blood-filled palms of concrete dreams. They save me, raise me and make me turn all the norms into their own headed storms.

His Dream Girl

The patterns of the winter rain reminds me
of the times I cry over you. Alone,
deeply rooted to the thoughts of
never being the girl of your dreams.

I am a damn fool for changing my soul with
shades of foundation, coral to the cheeks,
nudes to my lips and mascara to the lashes;
these were the kind of girls you
deeply admire.

Perhaps, I am blind but I swear to the stars
if the constellations align,
eternity is you for me.

But you settle for a dream girl that recites
those three words only when she
grows tired of being alone.

And you believe her...
every
    damn
        time.

Blood Beauty

In a field of red poppies,
they disguise the beauty of it's inked fragility.
It is said, even the birds and the bees
fear to steal treasures of their kingdom society.
Dear poison, dear poison,
what is forbidden is the fault of old traditions.
The city is greedy,
only opening the gates for the pretties.
In a field of red poppies, they disguise the beauty
as a cemetery for the uglies.

5:47a.m.

When the morning sun rises,
regret will climb into my body for refusing sleep.
The early summer breeze makes itself comfortable,
roams in the blinds of my windows and seeps into
my lonely atmosphere as I write this.
I'm wide awake because
oceans away—no, worlds away, you are.
The only sound heard is the train up north.
I wander over my dead body
if you've received my letters
and I know you don't
because I don't bother sending them.

Graves of Hybrids

Your native tongue
will bite you in the
chest.
A twist to your chained testicles
down to the books of your feet
will become
a bedded siren.
You will bleed and
chase for ears to
depict your air.
Cheers to the ones spoon-feeding you;
a recovery to amnesia and melancholic blues.

Buy What You Reap

We blame time and the interruptions in our life;
a reasoned confirmation to justify the company of
complications fabricated with reality.
And we believe that in its tick-tocking mutterings
comes the lack of preparation to—

Modern Lifetale

I used to believe that in happiness, it will flood through my
silhouette body for finding the love of my life. But you see,
it's a pass-down *myth* everyone claims to swallow down
their mind. No one talks about a love in the night, bloody
and chaste; only a reciprocation back with vain and manipulation.
In place and time, everything falls apart perfectly—piecing
nostalgia together to fall out of tricks. This is a modern lifetale
where full-time villains become heroes in the counts of
temporary heads in the future of our earth.

Asudem

She hibernates on false glorification.
Ships to her throne
comes farewells to clones.
She is wicked, magnificent, and graceful.
Curse her heart,
I warn you.
Listen to the venom speaking from her slaves;
indeed, you should protect yourself,
but you should know,
you'll still end up in your grave.

Body Vomit

Home.
Cut open to
remodel past histories
and glue puzzles in worn out clay.
Over and over and over,
I come up as an
eruption of fossils.
Each precious
discovery
is thousands of me,
a hostage.
It smells of sour milk,
inked with expired alphabets
that never got the
chance to
fully form words.

Our Safe Space

Across the timeline of the frame, the calendar is already 4 months old with 91 days in the counting to the new year. Considering that I lost you to trying since then, I expect myself to abandon the paradigm we were once rooted in. But, you're stuck to me like the stars displaying in the night sky. You still orbit my world, despite the empty space of it all. We were, indeed, a chaos in the making, footsteps with blueprints in each other's presence— behind wicked dreams and broken backs, each blood in the cut from the very existence of reality. In the age of time when we're not too late in the blooming and the constellations in your earth finally makes room for me, I hope gravity will have the power to pull us back together; someday, somehow.

Life's Best Enemy

Across from me sits all of the temporary
reality I used to be.
In time,
I begin reflecting
on menace personalities
around this city,
specifically my sanctuary.

I die at age five,
a recovery to life and
it's demeaning sanity.

Such innocence begins
ripping the skins of profanity
to feed armies
of teeth.

I have become the people I
preach not to be.

Across from here sits little old me

and she's the only one who deciphers
the grave of my tragedy.

Temporary Muse

Breathtaking,
indeed,
that I forgot it could
break my heart.

The Clash of Enmity

Arise,
from graves and stoned-written names.
You and I,
are lapses of flowers for the forgotten.
Let the triumph begin, a muse of fantasies;
once upon a time,
there were orange cotton skies and
souls that bleed nothing but golden crimes.
In a winter of spring,
calligraphy falls from limbs and roses
of cheeks.
Arise, child,
this is just the beginning.

Caged Mirage

I am only six years deep in the world of deceiving cheaps when the second house to the corner street becomes my home. Within the stages of flux, I am with unfortunate events; a dollhouse behind a caged mirage. Given to us is bits of unnerving beats and a vision full of common beasts to survive the battle fiend of luckless treasures. We were so busy with the mold of our pretentious acts with theatrical divinity that belief in this mystery, they did receive. Upon that comes paper people and their chainsaw hearts, fingers all on us; a refusal to understand the circumstances that we too, suffer from the start of time to the present of day. If being kind is a game of manipulation in return, certainly, we are shades of lesions, our own agony in disguise along with the roots of people's carelessness. If being candid is a crime, off with our heads for audacious reasonings, being decorations on sticks for a victory in the coming.

I am *only* six years young when these paper people began to ravage the second house to the corner street before it could even become my home.

Identity Theft

A room with laughter and careful sheep conversations
fills with eyes of dried-out streams,
preparing for a scripted life to accompany
the lively puppeted gleams.
Chained lips and clogged word vomits
like a chameleon who can't even commit.
May you find your clone
in this prototypical zone.

Meeting Another Earth

The clock misses its tick after midnight and before I know it, it's
already dead time. I am completely and utterly alone with my
army of thoughts and limbotic world inside of me. Unknowingly,
I have become the victim of my own life story. Rolling down
my cheekbones they go to the very ends of my facial structure
before they seep into my pillow. Karma hits me again, each day
in the counting and bargaining for others to pray them innocent
while attacking me; I am the only confirmed guilty. Did you
really want us to be a temporary memory stuck in the far ends of
our heads, only a retrace back to the break of seldomness?
Perhaps, our
sweet cruelty has judged me to be nothing more but a good
night for you and your life.

p.s. when the stars don't align and the world becomes
heavy with its broken pages, i hope you think of
me—someday, maybe when you realize we're both just
lonely and missing half of our body pieces in parts of us.

Battles of Cliché

Forever is an old tale to reason with the end.

Blood Bath

I rinse all of my pitiful scars and sins today.
Perhaps, it's a forlorn attempt because it's no
holy water to wipe away any
revolting win.

My consciousness deluge from a
painted-down face
I forgot to claim.

This body fuels up with fragility and muffled breaths.

In
and
out;

                              uneven of the unknown.

Light of ground
        yet heavy at heart.

Passage of People

I remind them that the presence of a friend is here but it is in the
    there they seek to reach.
Sleepless nights will eventually turn into long overdone novels to
    single words.
I taught myself to silence my worst enemies when they had me
    by the throat because you couldn't bear to see me burn.
My brown blinds soiled inside of me and on your leave, I seldom
    spoke of the bruises and blood in my palms to keep you from
    screaming.
You piece and fall apart in my presence, closer,
I pull you in,
and out, you stray away.

Death of an Artist

you rot of poetry.
　　　　pure, raw, intimacy.

City of Habits

The summer air let out hearts intertwining in
the midst of confessional season.
We write novels of each other, build plot
twists and structures
of characters we often bleed with.

But autumn is here to greet us
and end this myth.
As tragic as it sounds,
it makes sense that it did.

Copycat

Your words no longer seek curiosity of my existence that when your questions run wild to kill the silence now, I couldn't respond. I have long stopped being inquisitive about my well-being too.

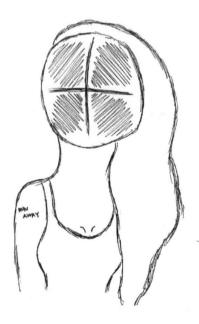

Armageddon

I hear the birds crying over my grave.
They sing a tale
that not even heaven
can sell.

Perhaps, I am not bone
and fleshed-down decay;
not fossils of a past mistake.

Why else would the coffins
around me
be awake?

Sudden Boundaries

I want to be a part of your life
and you simply just want me to stay.

Replica

It's a shame in how they act
and show themselves
behind the camera;
glam up to conceal
 their own skin and flesh.

Behind their mannequin personality,
their expensive eyes don't look at me.
I know better to not be like them,
yet they continue to expect a greet to ease reality.

But you see,
I'm no dog
and I don't obey
those who bark
for attention.

> — all this wishful thinking
> just to have you come out as a cliche.
> what a pity.

Better not Bitter

Amongst blankets of chaos and waves of riot,
I am expected to go on autopilot.
Kindman says to not let the world become bitter,
but better.

Perhaps, they are right, yet
I *am*
bitter and better
than ever.

Rage for Freedom

I am a creature,
four legs,
fur to the curve,
outside, in
and skin like fire.

My teeth are
strong enough
to tear bodies apart,
sadistic and
unapologetic for
a hungry heart.

Dolor

Look at the jade sky
then to the ground
beneath your bare feet.
My presence, darling,
will soon go missing
and here you are,
by my side, disappear.

Like the earth,
we crack and
consume
too much saltwater
tears.

Butterfly Effect

In a claustrophobic area, we cocoon in the windy trees of mother earth's broken limbs and natural disasters. Curiosity kills the dream-space we create towards the moon too soon—we end up like Icarus and his luckless wounds.

Isolated Ground

What is once a bond in the making becomes a tornado you slowly find escape from. I remember it all from the shy and careless fancies, a drive in our sanity to the edge of the world. We have a connection or so, I thought.

You plant nothing more than a temporary stop inside of me, map your next destination as I excuse your red flags to stay awhile longer. But each pinpointed mark you make needles my bones, in which burns worn out echoes. I am a mix signal for your presence to settle down, in no guarantee of a home being built in this isolated ground.

And that alone, is enough for you to pack up your bags, without another word said.

— We never gave each other a proper goodbye.
I wonder, does that mean we're still in each other's lives?

Until Next Spring

Like cherry blossoms in the spring,
we dance in the wind and
kiss the graves of the earth
as if we were
soulmates;
a match made-up in purgatory.
We watch lovers bloom
in the ratings of their roots.
We were one.

But when winter comes,
every blossomed swain began to
wither and die.
And just like that,
we did too.
Until next spring,
my dearest love.

Army of Norms

In the threshold of my brain,
you step into the home of my head.
You govern my body,
hands on my teeth and down
to the very nooks of my sanctuary.
There, you rewrite
my madness
to receive your crown.

Funeral for the Mind

The typical 8 hours of dreams,
Oh, what a foolish nightmare they even bleed.
You will still awake, dead in defeat.
It will only engrave our body
to maintain concrete
pain and pills to resolve
our own thrills.

Diagnose me,
unknown?
Check me,
anybody.
Please,
End me.

Mother Earth's Sixth Sense

It's a love like this that the Gods and Hybrids envy.
They let the ocean come, overruling day and night.

Distance
          Space
                  Stardust

Will you still love me in the arms of Death and his
awfully romantic parts?

Body Language

I am the cavity you pull out,
the skin deep you hate
in starvation for
a classic petite waste.

The message you neglect,
your response only for
infatuated recognition.

An irrelevant extra
in the ambiance
of your
main clique.

Let me rip you out
and make myself
the lead
to watch *you*
bleed.

The Wolf and His Star

People talk so much about the sun and moon that they forget
about the wolf and his star.
The wolf and his star?

I have a theory. I believe that in the olden days, there is only one
star and she chose the wolf as her dearest lover. But he let it all
go, says he believes that she deserves the galaxies and universe of
freedom. To this day, if you listen carefully, you can hear the
wolf crying his heart out to her. It is often said that his howls
were for the moon but truth be told, his anger rises when he
finds his star in mulch like gold to the wholesome sky and his
careless decision. Apparently in the dark, she shines in every
aspect of his world, brighter than anything else beyond his earth.
Everyone applauds and awakens for the night show, thanks him
for reasons to live and create. But you see, the sky does not love
her. He is in love with the way people make him feel; too much,
maybe, that he tears every inch of her apart, disperse the kingdom
of his firmament—he shines brightly in the ghost town of his
empty, cold-headed heart.

Perhaps, that is the same with us. We love the ones we cannot
have and sometimes there's nothing we could do about it but
bruise each time we see them falling apart.

Tainted Dollface

I paint my own masks, conceal my passings
and a smolder facade.
Each burial comes for the person I make,
brain full of tin and a hollow heart
always for the end.
Apply numbing cream to
patients in the waiting and
hammer their eyes with needles,
open.

We suffer everywhere we go.
This gift from me to you;
let me, darling,
sew your pretty cornered lips to
your porcelain cheeks.
Deceive everyone you may please
with a teaspoon of
chameleon tease.

Deja Vu

It's not love. It's not love. It's. not. love.

I keep a 95 month old mantra in the windows of my head that in
my oblivious days, love is not what seeps through the heavens of
my sky. I am too young then to even label it anything but a
temporary fancy. Sadly, it's been eight years and god, I still can't
talk about you without hearing the ambulance in my throat and
feeling my brown orbs compete against the rumbling rainstorm
building up inside of me.

Time will heal. Time will heal. Time will heal.

I've given time so much of my trust
                but why am I still so damn broken?

Chasing Dreamers

Don't chase after your dreams,
let your dreams chase you.

Collided Calamities

I die every time reality lays its fate on me,
but my sanity lives in the fancies
of your menace existence.
Our souls will diverge underneath soils
and dirt of the palsy humus, yet,
your hymn will muse through my broken carcasses
and I'll remember you within every fragment inside of me.

"I don't want to be with you,"
Your voice mimics my trials of
false hope and exultant tears,
"What are two broken souls to do
with each other?"
Your eyes glister with nothing
more than silent infatuation,
"We'll never stop falling apart, darling—"
You wait.

You wait for some sort of epiphany, but—
void in cosmos just isn't enough.

For The Stars They Stole from Me

In a meadow of prosy forget-me-nots,
fire seldom kisses the rain.

One, in peace.
Two, for goodbye.

Here comes our freedom,
a sacrifice to no longer dream.

For your dear life,
please   forget   me.

Burned Headed Souls

I am not a single personality soul.
I am a creation upon depths of destruction
that has aged from years ago to
the present of time, still proceeding.
I will ruin you; I've already
destroyed myself.

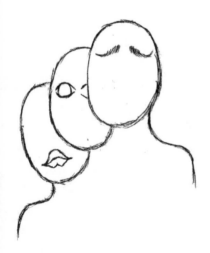

Ground Zero

Hands, homeless in foreign lands
were an exchange for artificial grands.

Legs soar caverned rocks
and up gag machine-clocks.

His visions blur with cocaine features,
scatters with dreams and hidden liquor.

She cages her life on patience,
saves face from traditional violence.

They were puzzles like their infants,
wed at child commitment,
possibly wanting to cut
their own guts.

Crowned Norns

In chronological crimes,
the first isn't the worse,
the second isn't the best
and the third is anonymous.
Be in gratitude,
your hands did not meet
with a half reciprocate wanderer.
You are scarred, crush to molds,
crack to nothing and
a savior to self-destruction.
Run, you fool,
This isn't the only cheap fate
that will stop them
from being cruel.

Follow Forbid Forget

In a universe parallel to earth's duty,
we'll play our final show.

Not light of tragedy and remorse,
but in dark timely trained chastity.

Let intertwined hands speak a whisper.

Follow the dead night whistles,
forbid a kiss with our locked eyes,
forget the graves calling us craze.

I'll take the fallen pits of our countless sins,
and allow skeletons to peel my skin.

This place isn't y(ours); years
in the making cannot bring me back to the
living.

My dear, even the moon has
disappeared.

Earth in Dreamland

The cities here are shield sheets,
a fabrication with blue printed criminals
and out dated missing souls.
There lives a girl,
eyes cut out,
loved by a kidnapper;
better to have known duties
to keep her locks caged.
Beneath the surface of her
callous crumb feet
peels upon windows of burnt teeth
and old clues,
unfinished
for her juvient
years.

Farewell to Naiveness

I erase the painful memories and keep our reveries in my headspace, a temporary bliss now. I don't think of you as often anymore but there are nights where I do see you in my dreams, regret and asking for time to slow down for us to start over again. It's funny because the person you are in my sleep will never conform to who you are in the present day. I just hope you don't carry pain around anymore as an excuse to stay away from people and I hope you are well.

Speaking Sirens

I speak but don't talk.
I listen but can't hear.
I am unfathomable.
Knot my toes with building blocks
and tangle my guts with clocks.
Fuck it,
tick it to doomsday.
Unlike you, I prepare
for this getaway,
What else do *you* have to say?

The Blame We Pay

They keep saying that love leaves;
it takes two people to deplete.
Judge rules,
confirm deceit.
Love does not leave.
Tug and pull,
they'll still account you
for things you've already
upheave.
It's our call,
darling.
Don't you get it?
Love did not leave,
people do.

The Mad Hatter's Picasso

I've been a wanderer in the Mad Hatter's land.
His coy aptitude paints wholeheartedly
on blank sheeps
with blood wine,
each from another person's weep.

Adore he, I did.
So I give myself to him in three:
a heart, a mind, a body;
indeed, his cup of tea.

Three Eyes, One Voice

I wear a gown in sleeves
of thick skin
and abandon the
therapeutic emotional cry.

Bathe in gray noise,
eat mud cakes
and decaying
old aches.

One should know better than to
spare my feelings
to keep me healing.

You're such a sweetheart
for even caring.
But I don't need a coward
kidding themselves in shields
when long ago,
to this day,
I *am* the battlefield.

Candid Kills

They were comfortable with the silence of my words, their *truth* for me.

But once I finally broke out of shadows and overdue lies, suddenly, they couldn't understand me anymore.

The Devil's Plan

constellations upon roots of stars,
not for me but for you.

       blood and sins consecrate me
of convictions and reveries.

retreat they say,
but i continue to sleep.

Road to Tranquility

I am the silence people try to kill with
meaningless fancies that lead to

nowhere.

Bottled Covet

I remember telling you that I am bad luck when it comes to love.
I am always on a one-sided trail and if not, something; anything
always waves in between me and the off-cut string attached to
the reciprocate being.

Eventually, we come to a halt of more than friends. Despite the
distance, our conversations make you very much present with
me.

> Remember when our fancies began dancing and flirting
> amongst the stars in the depths of god knows where?

> If things had turned out differently,
> do you think we could've lived
> the future we burn into our brains?

Truth be told, I wish we were selfish enough to break the stigma
of reality.
But the only reality I live in now is that I am in fact, very much
bad luck when it comes to love.

California Dreaming

I have been a challenge with
swords thrown at my face.

All this poetry and
non-existence forming
a body space.

Black Out Days

I'm forgetting.
My memories 24 hours ago
are difficult to retrace back to.

Perhaps, my brain is bleeding
of long ago beatings.

Whatever it is, muse does not come,
and my heart isn't pleasing.

I was okay all my 18 years of living,
yet 2 years too deep got me fleeting.

This must be aging
or life is slowly
fading.

Common Dreamcatchers

In my dreams,
I send you a farewell today.
I write a story,
about you; about us
like how we did, so damn long ago.
Reality climbs in and kisses us with
a life we once
took compromise in.

But we both know too well,
that's not how this story goes.

I awake this time and
perhaps, it is your way of
saying goodbye.

Upon the Falling

I wait.
Wait upon heavenly bodies;
wait in the antecedent of portend time.
But fate dances prudently
and relinquishes.

1,397 MI

We talk a lot about the grounds of the sky and the pin-pointed stars. Often far away; seldom spoke where we'd be as long as we have each other. I've never been too fond of facts, but I'd listen to your tangents about cosmos and admire how excitement climbs out of you just to speak of it and I, to hear your voice echo the halls of my mind.

You'll listen to my magical realism, claims of fictional creatures in the gates of inception; secret code names to disguise the fact that I've been talking about you this whole time. Perhaps, I am too much in love with fabrications of myths and olden tales but you don't mind it because you know damn well, you're thinking about us too.

But we stopped talking about it after that rainstorm.

I still think of you,
      and I miss you.

WANTED

I think it is quite obvious that I am your wanted villain.
You cuff-hand my paper tongue and jail it for weakness.

Therapy with Death

When a calling comes to an end,
save all choke up silence in
a covet chest.

Words will no longer be valid;
a language barrier to the
living and the dead.

If thoughts are only to be sold
only at the fall of graves,
do not mask in grief and regret;
tears should only be in place
of those circling around
your earth.

Because clearly,
what is once in existence
is not in the hands of
your matter at all.

Red String of Fate

I hear stories about the red string of fate; no matter how close it is to breaking apart, you and your soulmate are bound to find each other, always. And I suppose it's true but I also believe that we all have different kinds of soulmates.

The soulmate you almost end up with.
The soulmate that wrecks you.
The soulmate you let go.
The soulmate you never got to meet.
The soulmate that meets someone else.
The soulmate that time couldn't promise.
The soulmate that is never yours to keep in the beginning.
The soulmate you didn't love back.
The soulmate you miss.

So tell me, how can I find—

Glass Face

If you want to destroy,
your granted wish
masks her.

Ultraviolence

She rises into love,
blushing of cheek scarlet;
too much, perhaps
that the sun flourishes roses
all around his space.
A thing or two,
the beloved cracks
earth suddenly ablazes.
Shelters become ashes upon dirt,
feeding greens that will,
in seconds,
kill their roots.
If in fact,
love does not kill,
why are millions
on their
last breath?

Finale

Eye sockets ricochet down
to earth.
Fistful pens bleed inked blues,
on torn papers and rooted truths.
Heavy, not shoulders, not feet,
but greed.

It drives, destination on its own:
Create, rev, fright,
but truthfully this isn't the one.
Cross out characters.
Scratch faces.
Serve bloodshed tools.
Torn and piece.
Bury
Revive
Alive

People only seek performance,
never behind the curtains.

Buried With The Truth

I watch you dig your own grave,
sulk when the fireworks scream our fate.

This isn't a match in our mind,
a cross-dressing in a close case.

Unknown to me,
you push and fell,
I, in your
place.

Erase your name, you did
and carve my initials
into the abyss.

A Letter From the Ends of the Earth

To my dearest beloved ones, I cannot take you with me this time and for this, forgive me for not fighting against Death and his arranging madness. I will be locked out of life; a jail from the forbiddenness to ever be in the threshold of the oxygen in-take I have taken for granted. The ocean won't wave into the spaces between my toes anymore and I'll forget my home bodies and cities of strangers that were once a hybrid of unconditional love. My muse, my dreams, my tough luck will no longer linger in the depths of my thoughts. My errs will go with me; I won't excuse myself of my wrong doings. Deepest apologies to those unfinished conversations and wishful vacations. My story will end here and the cycle of life will exchange my goneness in a form of birth and new revelations. I will lose myself and the being I am in this given lifetime. I will forget the faces of those who raised me in the showers of April and continue to strengthen me with my tigress trait. I will not remember those who I have hurt and brought nothing but trails of disappointment and unexplained leavants. I will not recall my first heartbreak and how karma has chased after me, time and time again, only to temporary bliss; a life of always giving more than receiving. Forget me not but don't think of me often; a part of me will always be with you, no matter where you are.

Splintered Pleasures

Upon the calling of flux,
my aching home will scream your name
and the habits of your finished cigarettes
will eradicate me to peace.

Blood Moon

I light and grey the ashes
found in your routine.
A hybrid you are;
five leaf clover on my jeans.
I shed like smoke,
a breath of freshly pluck
thorns,
leaving splinters
on your bloody fingertips.
Metallic,
you taste between my teeth
but lucky for you,
it only happens during an
eclipse.

Untold Realization

My love, my love, my love.
These flowers of fancies
will dance upon skins and bones,
bleeding myself dry with blood.

Pursuit of Broken Breaths

We bleed the same
and yet you fixate
our hurting,
claiming that I left
unharmed.

— often enough, the end comes sooner
than it should.

there is no beginning to look back at,
you were already at the finish line
with me.

Solace & Her Witnesses

A battle cry broke through the essence of these long-overdue
critiques. We fought through old mazes that lead back to the very
beginning of its entrance; a circle of overweight loathing. It isn't
then, did I realize that I have become a bully to my
wretchedness; a coward, begging for answers that even my
silhouettes in the moment could not fathom. My sanctuary,
neither full or empty,
overflows with zest of pleading deaths
without even speaking.
Had I not stayed awake in the depths of
my orange cotton daze at
that time in my life, I would not be here,
telling you this tale.

Acknowledgements

First things first, if you made it to the very nook of these pages in your hands, my gratification is forever in the arms of your existence. To even think that one person seeks to find what my mind can craft or want to experience my turn of the universe is insane. With your willingness to open up this book, able to indulge and collide into the power of language, I truly do feel at ease.

To my family, I cannot express how incredibly lucky I am to have you all as a support system, disciplining me with tough love. You are my backbone. Near or far, you know who you are.

To my friends, I hope you're all well and living the life that you've envisioned. Please never give up and always have courage.

To Mr. Jensen, for giving my creation in the making, then, a look. I appreciate every amount of given criticism you've given me into consideration to better my pieces. I cannot thank you enough.

Shout out to my big sister Linda Vang for making the beautiful art cover. It was nice merging my words to your artistic mind and seeing both of our ideas come to life.

Special thanks to Atmosphere Press and their hard working team for wanting to make this a reality. I am finally my dream person and you made that happen. My journey starts here, and I wouldn't have wanted it any other way.

To me, writing since 5 years young, creating scenarios, making imaginations, inking fanfiction and scribbling everything on pieces of paper, you made it. You finally got to witness yourself come this far in life to be the author you always wanted to be.

About Atmosphere Press

Atmosphere Press is an independent, full-service publisher for excellent books in all genres and for all audiences. Learn more about what we do at atmospherepress.com.

We encourage you to check out some of Atmosphere's latest releases, which are available at Amazon.com and via order from your local bookstore:

Grafting, poetry by Amy Lundquist

How to Hypnotize a Lobster, poetry by Kristin Rose Jutras

Love is Blood, Love is Fabric, poetry by Mary De La Fuente

The Mercer Stands Burning, poetry by John Pietaro

Lovely Dregs, poetry by Richard Sipe

Meraki, poetry by Tobi-Hope Jieun Park

Calls for Help, by Greg T. Miraglia

Out of the Dark, poetry by William Guest

Lost in the Greenwood, poetry by Ellen Roberts Young

Blessed Arrangement, poetry by Larry Levy

Shadow Truths, poetry by V. Rendina

A Synonym for Home, poetry by Kimberly Jarchow

Big Man Small Europe, poetry by Tristan Niskanen

The Cry of Being Born, poetry by Carol Mariano

Lucid_Malware.zip, poetry by Dylan Sonderman

In the Cloakroom of Proper Musings, by Kristin Moriconi

It's Not About You, poetry by Daniel Casey

The Unordering of Days, poetry by Jessica Palmer

Radical Dances of the Ferocious Kind, poetry by Tina Tru

The Woods Hold Us, poetry by Makani Speier-Brito

About the Author

Eenam Vang was born in Sacramento, California in the spring of 1998. She finds it quite essential to slow down and admire the little things in life. Creating fantasy out of the ordinary, she is driven by the light of imagination into the corners of her head. Besides writing and reading, Eenam finds herself most content spending time with family, enjoying coffee, listening to vinyl, the color orange, and dancing.

For more, follow her on social media:
Instagram: eenamvang

CPSIA information can be obtained
at www.ICGtesting.com
Printed in the USA
LVHW091204150721
692784LV00008B/995

9 781637 528372